A NEW IMAGE

BY
CAROL L. BRIGGS

Copyright © 2021 by Carol L. Briggs

All rights reserved. This book or any portion thereof may not be reproduced or transmitted in any form or manner, electronic or mechanical, including photocopying, recording, or by any information storage or retrieval system, without the express written permission of the copyright owner except for the use of brief quotations in a book review or other noncommercial uses permitted by copyright law.

Printed in the United States of America

Library of Congress Control Number: 2020920789
ISBN: Softcover   978-1-64908-851-2
        eBook   978-1-64908-850-5

Republished by: PageTurner Press and Media LLC
Publication Date: 03/09/2021

To order copies of this book, contact:

PageTurner Press and Media
Phone: 1-888-447-9651
order@pageturner.us
www.pageturner.us

A Thought for you, the Reader...

Wouldn't it be exciting to change our worldly, worn-out image into a brand-new personality and physical appearance?

No matter how much we try to stick to a healthy diet, exercise regimen, and/or a genuine, sincere attitude change, we can't seem to persevere long enough to accomplish our long-term goal—or even a short-term goal.

This book gives us a solution to our woes--one "mysterious" word found in this audio will solve our problems…AND, will also pique our interest about how others have found The Way to A NEW IMAGE—which isn't really new, but "called back" into the image in which we were born.

Being "Born Again" gives us a "new beginning" in the Image of Yeshua. (the first few lines of the song come on after the reader gives the title and author and thought)

This audio book is a shortened version of the original book A NEW IMAGE-- Imago Dei…

In the physical book you will be able to walk in the sandals of Noah, Joseph, Moses, and Joshua—all foreshadowing the image of Yeshua. (two more lines of song…then: Reader begins:

Now!... you must forget "you" and put yourself in the sandals of Moses (Moshe)…in your prime at 80 years old. You are tending the flock of your father-in-law, Jethro, the priest of Midian, dealing with a "first-time" mama sheep, when you hear a voice calling your name. It seems to be coming from a bush that is on fire but not being consumed.

1

'Moses, Moses!" a great booming voice came from the bush. I said, **"Hineni!"** (Here am I.)

'Do not draw near this place. Take your sandals off your feet, for the place where you stand is holy ground. I am the God of your father—the God of Abraham, the God of Isaac, and the God of Jacob.' (NKJV, Exodus 3:4, 5, 6) I hid my face, 'cause I knew if I looked upon God, I would die.

'I have surely seen the oppression of My people who are in Egypt, and have heard their cry because of their taskmasters, for I know their sorrows. So I have come down to deliver them out of the hand of the Egyptians, and to bring them up from that land to a good and large land, to a land flowing with milk and honey, to the place of the Canaanites and the Hittites and the Amorites and the Perizzites and the Hivites and the Jebusites.

Now, therefore, behold, the cry of the children of Israel has come to Me, and I have also seen the oppression with which the Egyptians oppress them. Come now, therefore, and I will send you to Pharaoh that you may bring my people, the children of Israel, out of Egypt.' (NKJV, Exodus 3:7-11) P.1 -359 wrds

I answered God, **"Who am I that I should go to Pharaoh, and that I should bring the children of Israel out of Egypt?"** (NKJV, Exodus 3:11)

God knew that I had killed that cruel Egyptian 40 years ago, and even though many of the people who were hunting for me at that time have died, one might still be alive.

Besides, **"O my Lord, I am not eloquent, neither before nor since You have spoken to Your servant; but I am slow of speech and slow of tongue."** (NKJV, Ex.4:10)

So the Lord said to me, **'Who has made man's mouth? Or Who makes the mute, the deaf, the seeing, or the blind? Have not I, the Lord? Now therefore, go and I will be with your mouth and teach you what you shall say.'** (NKJV, Ex. 4:11, 12)

I again asked the Lord to send someone else. He became very angry with me, scaring the living daylights out of me. So, when He said I could use Aaron the Levite, my brother, for my mouthpiece; my Lord telling me what to tell Aaron; and that He would be with me and teach me what I shall do, I left Mt. Horeb, lamenting the day I had brought our flocks to the back of the desert wilderness that led to that Mountain. Zipporah had warned me about that mountain--her people had often seen smoke and fire up there, and no one ever ventured too close to what they called "the Mountain of God." Of course, that had just made me more curious.

In hindsight, of course, I now know all of my childhood experiences growing up as the son of an Egyptian princess; then, after having killed an Egyptian who was beating my Hebrew brother, I had to run to the desert to hide; so, became a shepherd for Jethro, the Midian priest, who gave me his daughter, Zipporah, in marriage. No wonder God was so mad at me...He had been preparing me for this job for many years, from the time Jochebed, my Hebrew mother, had put me in the tiny ark made of reeds and pitch to save me from death at the hands of Pharaoh's "flunkies" until the day I came to the burning bush which never burned up. All of what happens on this earth and in heaven is a plan put into effect before creation--by our Almighty God (Adonai, Elohim)--God the Father, the Son, and the Holy Spirit (The Ruach Hachedesh.)

What a God!

I believed God. If He said He would give me the words to tell Aaron what he needed to say to my people, Israel, being oppressed there in Egypt, and the other words to tell Pharaoh besides, "Let My people go!;" then, I will be able to face the man who is considered the greatest man in this known world (by other men, of course, not by our Adonai, Who is our Creator; and Who had put the Pharaoh into his position in the first place.)

With I AM WHO I AM behind me, what can Pharaoh do to me when God says, **'See, I have made you as God to Pharaoh, and Aaron your brother shall be your prophet. You shall speak all that I command you. And Aaron your brother shall tell Pharaoh to send the children of Israel out of his land.'** (NKJV, Exodus 7:1, 2)

Aaron and I went to Pharaoh and did as Adonai commanded...Aaron threw down his staff before Pharaoh and before his servants, and it became a serpent.

Then Pharaoh called for the wise men and the sorcerers, and they too, the magicians of Egypt, did the same with their secret arts. For each man threw down his staff, and they became serpents. But Aaron's staff swallowed up their staffs. Yet Pharaoh's heart was

hardened. So he did not listen to them—just as Adonai had said. (MJFB, Exodus 7:11-13)

Then came the first plague: Try to imagine all the people in Egypt seeing their main source of water, the Nile, red with blood… **'Take your rod and stretch out your hand over the waters of Egypt, over their streams, over their rivers, over their ponds, and over all their pools of water, that they may become blood. And there shall be blood throughout all the land of Egypt, both in buckets of wood and pitchers of stone.' The fish that were in the river died, the river stank, and the Egyptians could not drink the water of the river. So there was blood throughout all the land of Egypt. Then the Magicians of Egypt did so with their enchantments; and Pharaoh's heart grew hard, and he did not heed them, as the Lord had said.** (NKJV, Exodus 7: 19, 21, 22)

For the second plague, God said to me to tell Pharaoh that if he didn't let His people go, **'Behold, I will smite all your territory with frogs. So the river shall bring forth frogs abundantly, which shall go up and come into your house, into your bedroom, on your bed, into the houses of your servants, on your people, into your ovens, and into your kneading bowls.'** (NKJV, Exodus 8:2,3)

After Pharaoh's magicians did so with their enchantments, and brought up frogs on the land of Egypt, Pharaoh begged us to take away the frogs and he would let the people go.

But when Pharaoh saw that there was relief, he hardened his heart and did not listen to them—just as Adonai had said. (MJFB Exodus 8:11)

The gnats of the third plague stumped Pharaoh's magicians, though, and they said to Pharaoh, **"This is the finger of God." But Pharaoh's heart was hardened, and he did not listen to them, just as Adonai had said."** (MJFB, Exodus 8: 15)

After the third, the plague of gnats, God said, '**And in that day I will set apart the land of Goshen, in which My people dwell, that no swarms of flies shall be there, in order that you may know that I am the Lord in the midst of the land. I will make a difference between My people and your people. Tomorrow this sign shall be.'"** (NKJV, Exodus 8: 22, 23)

Why did God allow those first three plagues to include us, His chosen people? I figure God had to wake up many of us from nearly 300+

years of forgetting to tell our children about the One True God of Abraham, Isaac, and Jacob. Because the generations were not reminded of their glorious Creator every day, the influence of Egyptian slave-masters demanding most of our time, and a myriad of man-made gods constantly talked about by the "wealthy, educated, privileged Egyptians," our people only knew what they saw and heard every day. When you are a slave, it is very simple to just comply and think about nothing except putting the next foot in front of the other.

So "out of sight, out of mind" through almost ten generations produced apathy in the lives of the Hebrew people since Joseph had died. Many had forgotten or never knew about the covenant God had made with Noah, also the covenant He made with Abraham. However, there was always a remnant of true believers!

These three plagues the children of Israel experienced served to demonstrate the glory of our God, Elohim--to give us a "fear" (respect) for the power and wonder of our Almighty God; and to convince the elders I was not trying to take over their jobs, but just complete the job Adonai had given me and groomed me for since before time.... to lead His chosen people, the children of Israel, out of the bonds of slavery.....(just as Jesus, Yeshua, our Jewish Savior, saves us out of the bonds of slavery to sin.)

The fourth plague–flies--struck with a vengeance. **Thick swarms of flies came into the house of Pharaoh, into his servant's houses, and into the land of Egypt. The land was corrupted because of the swarms of flies.** (NKJV, Exodus 8:24)

Pharaoh then told me we could go and sacrifice to our God in the land. However, I had to say "No!" to that because, **"If we sacrifice the abomination of the Egyptians before their eyes, then will they not stone us?"** (NKJV, Exodus 8:26b)

"I will let you go, that you may sacrifice to the Lord your God in the wilderness; only you shall not go very far away. Intercede for me." (NKJV, Exodus 8: 28.)

As usual, Pharaoh dealt deceitfully with us after the Lord had done according to the word of Moses when he interceded for Pharaoh.

'Behold, the hand of the Lord will be on your cattle in the field, on the horses, on the donkeys, on the camels, on the oxen, and on the sheep—a very severe pestilence. And the Lord will make a difference between the livestock of Israel and the livestock of

Egypt. So nothing will die of all that belongs to the children of Israel.' (NKJV, Exodus 9: 3, 4) Even after this fifth plague, the heart of Pharaoh remained hard and he did not let the people go.

The next one, #6, God said to Aaron and me, **'Take for yourselves handfuls of ashes from a furnace, and let Moses scatter it toward the heavens in the sight of Pharaoh. And it will become fine dust in all the land of Egypt, and it will cause boils that break out in sores on man and beast throughout all the land of Egypt.'**

Even though pharaoh's magicians could not stand before me because of the boils, the Lord hardened the heart of Pharaoh, and he did not heed them.

The Lord said to Pharaoh, 'As yet you exalt yourself against my people in that you will not let them go. Behold, tomorrow about this time, I will cause very heavy hail to rain down, such as has not been in Egypt since its founding until now.' (NKJV, Exodus 9:8, 9, 11, 12, 17, 18)

We had reminded Pharaoh and his people to flee into their houses and put their livestock there as well; those who feared the word of the lord, after seeing and experiencing six plagues, realized God kept His Word and they obeyed. However, those who didn't believe God were wiped out because...

... the Lord sent thunder and hail, and fire darted to the ground, and the Lord rained hail on the land of Egypt. And the hail struck throughout the whole land of Egypt, all that was in the field, both man and beast; and the hail struck every herb of the field and broke every tree of the field. Only in the land of Goshen, where the children of Israel were, there was no hail. (NKJV, Exodus 9: 23, 25, 26)

I knew Pharaoh did not yet fear the Lord, but, after going out of the city, I spread out my hands to the Lord for the thunder and the hail to cease...

Again the Lord said to me, **'Go in to Pharaoh, for I have hardened his heart and the hearts of his servants, that I may show these signs of Mine before him. And that you may tell in the hearing of your son and your son's son** (this includes daughters also) **the mighty things I have done in Egypt, and My signs which I have done among them, that you may know that I am the Lord.'** (NKJV, Exodus 10:1, 2) (my parenthesis)

Comments by Charles Stanley on this verse—"God works His wonders not only so that unbelievers might see His power and repent and believe, but also so that His own people might remember His glory and so remain loyal to Him." (NKJV, Page 75.)

So we came once more to Pharaoh, for the eighth time, and said to him, **"Thus says the Lord God of the Hebrews: 'How long will you refuse to humble yourself before Me? Let My people go, that they may serve Me. Or else, if you refuse to let My people go, behold, tomorrow I will bring locusts into your territory."** (NKJV, Exodus 10: 3,4).

Pharaoh's heart again being hardened by God, Pharaoh agreed--but only to the men going—not the women and children and livestock.

(Partial obedience is unacceptable to our Almighty God!)

The locusts came the next morning, on the east wind that had blown all that day and all that night. **For they covered the face of the whole earth, so that the land was darkened; and they ate every herb of the land and all the fruit of the trees which the hail had left. So there remained nothing green on the trees or on the plants of the field throughout all the land of Egypt.** (NKJV, Exodus 10: 15)

When the Lord hardened Pharaoh's heart again after he had begged me to entreat the Lord to get rid of those locusts, which the Lord did with a very strong west wind....blew the locusts into the Red Sea; he, Pharaoh still did not let the Children of Israel go...so....

The ninth plague, the thick darkness they could actually feel, lasted for three days without respite. **They did not see one another; nor did anyone rise from his place for three days. But all the children of Israel had light in their dwellings.** (NKJV, Exodus 10: 23)

This time when I wouldn't agree to Pharaoh's stipulation that we could go, but couldn't take our herds and flocks, Pharaoh said to me, **'Get away from me! Take heed to yourself and see my face no more! For in the day you see my face you shall die!'**

Then the Lord said to me, **'I will bring one more plague on Pharaoh and on Egypt. Afterward he will let you go from here. When he lets you go, he will surely drive you out of here altogether. Speak now in the hearing of the people, and let every man ask from his neighbor and every woman from her neighbor, articles of silver and** articles of gold. And the Lord gave the people favor in the sight of the Egyptians.'** (NKJV, Exodus 11: 1-3)

The Egyptians not only gave favor to all of the children of Israel, they treated me as if I were great in their sight, especially the servants of Pharaoh. I found it difficult to make them see all of these miracles (plagues) and signs came from the One True God, the God of our fathers Abraham, Isaac, and Jacob.

The final devastation came when the first-born of all Egyptian families and of their animals, were struck dead:

"And thus you shall eat it (the Passover Lamb): with a belt on your waist, your sandals on your feet, and your staff in your hand. So you shall eat it in haste. It is the Lord's Passover. For I will pass through the land of Egypt on that night, and will strike all the firstborn in the land of Egypt, both men and beast; and against all the gods of Egypt I will execute judgment. I am the Lord. Now the blood (of the Passover Lamb—symbol of Jesus who became the Lamb of salvation) shall be a sign for you on the houses where you are. And when I see the blood, I will pass over you; and the plague shall not be on you to destroy you when I strike the land of Egypt." (My parenthesis)

Then, Pharaoh, who had lost his first-born son, called for Aaron and me by night and told us, **'Rise, go out from among my people, both you and the children of Israel. And go, serve the Lord as you have said.. Also take your flocks and your herds, as you have said, and be gone: and bless me also.'** (NKJV, Exodus 12: 31,32)

We didn't waste any time! We weren't sure how long the Egyptian people would be urging us to leave with all their trinkets of gold and silver they had pressed upon us as they were "pushing us out the door" so to speak. There was no time to make bread, **having their kneading bowls bound up in their clothes on their shoulders. And they baked unleavened cakes of the dough which they had brought out of Egypt; for it was not leavened, because they were driven out of Egypt and could not wait, nor had they prepared provisions for themselves.** (NKJV, Exodus 12:34, 39)

When we finally moved all of those thousands of people, as well as their herds and flocks, as far as the Red Sea, and camped before Pi Hahiroth, between Migdol and the sea, opposite Baal Zephon, we kneeled in prayer together to praise Him and thank Him for His abundant blessings, and to ask for further directions, especially since our last group had sent a messenger down to us saying much dust was showing in the sky moving toward us—seems to be many chariots riding full force coming up on our left flank.

Not a good sign—I <u>thought</u> they might regret losing all the free slave labor. At any rate, it was said that almost immediately, the Egyptians said, '**Why have we done this, that we have let Israel go from serving us?**' (NKJV, Exodus 14: 5b)

God told me to say to the people, **"Do not be afraid. Stand still, and see the salvation of the Lord, which He will accomplish for you today. For the Egyptians whom you see today, you shall see again no more forever. The Lord will fight for you, and you shall hold your peace."**

(music comes up a louder for about 60 seconds, then softens)

God said to me, 'Why do you cry to me? Tell the children of Israel to go forward. But lift up your rod, and stretch out your hand over the sea and divide it. And the children of Israel shall go on dry ground through the midst of the sea.' (NKJV, Exodus 14: 13-16)

The children of Israel obeyed with alacrity, walking all night to get the huge numbers of people, animals, and belongings across that dry land before the morning watch.

And the angel of God, who went before the camp of Israel, moved and went behind them; and the pillar of cloud went from before them and stood behind them. So it came between the camp of the Egyptians and the camp of Israel. Thus it was a cloud and darkness to the one, and it gave light by night to the other, so that the one did not come near the other all that night. (NKJV, Exodus 14:19, 20)

(music louder for another 40 seconds or so)

Now it came to pass, in the morning watch, that the Lord looked down upon the army of Egyptians through the pillar of fire and cloud, and He troubled the army of the Egyptians. And He took off their chariot wheels, so that they drove with difficulty; and the Egyptians said, 'Let us flee from the face of Israel, for the Lord fights for them against the Egyptians.' (NKJV, Exodus 14:24, 25)

(louder music)

When the Lord told me to stretch out my hand over the sea again, I obeyed Him immediately; and the waters came back upon the Egyptians, on their chariots, and on their horsemen. **So the Lord overthrew the Egyptians in the midst of the sea.** (NKJV, Exodus 14: 27b)

(crashing music)

Thus the Lord saved Israel that day from the hand of the Egyptians, and Israel saw the Egyptians dead on the seashore. Israel saw the great power that the Lord used against the Egyptians, so the people feared the Lord, and they believed in the Lord and in His servant Moses. (ESV, Exodus 14: 30, 31)

Reader says: Then Moses and the people of Israel sang this song to the Lord:

(about 2 or 3 minutes of music from Song of Moses I sent you.)

(After the music, finishes, resume reading...)

Then we all, a mixed multitude, journeyed from Rameses to Succoth.

We took a round-about route to get where God wanted us, but so far, no army has come against us. When I consider the route God gave us, He thinks of everything—we had no warriors yet; all of these people might have turned back to Egypt if they had met an army. As it was, our young men could train to be more aggressive during those times when they needed something to use up their excess energy.

I once more reminded the children of Israel, "Obedience brings blessings; disobedience brings curses." I'm sorry to say many forgot these important words on our way to the Promised Land.

While I was 40 days and 40 nights on the mountain talking with the Lord, the people grew impatient, persuaded Aaron, my brother, a priest of our Holy God, into fashioning a golden calf which they could worship as God until I came back—if I came back—they said, "He is probably dead by now."

When the Lord said to me, "**Go, get down! For your people whom you brought out of the land of Egypt have corrupted themselves. They have turned aside quickly out of the way which I commanded them. They have made themselves a molded calf, and worshiped it and sacrificed to it, and said 'This is your god, O Israel, that brought you out of the land of Egypt!' I have seen this people, and indeed it is a stiff-necked people!'** (NKJV, Exodus 32:7-9)

Distractedly thinking about how God had pointedly called them "your" people this time instead of "His" people, I hurriedly brought the tablets of stone down the mountain; and when I viewed their idolatry, my anger was so great that I flung down the tablets with God's commandments on them; and broke them there, at the foot of the mountain.

I ground that golden calf idol into powder, added water and made them drink it. Once more I went up to commune with the Lord, and pleaded with Him not to destroy all of this people when God had said, **'Now, therefore, let Me alone, that My wrath may burn hot against them and I may consume them. And I will make of you a great nation.'** (NKJV, Exodus 32:10)

But, I had begged, **"Lord, why does Your wrath burn hot against Your people whom You have brought out of the land of Egypt with great power and with a mighty hand? Why should the Egyptians speak and say, 'He brought them out to harm them, to kill them in the mountains, and to consume them from the face of the earth? Turn from Your fierce wrath, and relent from this harm to Your people."** (NKJV, Exodus 32:11-13)

So the Lord relented from the harm which He said He would do to His people. (NKJV, Exodus 32:14)

After more of the groanings and complainings, and now the golden calf, the Lord told me to separate the sheep from the goats, so I announced, **"Whoever is on the Lord's side—come to me!" And all the sons of Levi gathered themselves together to him."** (NKJV, Exodus 32:26)

Then I said to them, **"Thus says the Lord God of Israel; 'Let every man put his sword on his side, and go in and out from entrance to entrance throughout the camp, and let every man kill his brother, every man his companion, and every man his neighbor.' So the sons of Levi did according to the word of Moses. And about three thousand men of the people fell that day.** (NKJV, Exodus 33:27, 28)

Thank You, Lord for 120 years of a full life with guidance from you, especially when You chose me to lead Your people out of a life of slavery. Thank You for giving me a last commission to ordain Joshua with words from You in front of the whole multitude— **...charge Joshua, and encourage and strengthen him, for he shall go over at the head of this people, and he shall put them in possession of the land that you shall see.'** (ESV, Deuteronomy 3:28)

Then there will be no question about who is to be their leader! I realize the consequence from those two instances when I let anger cloud my mission is why I won't be able to live long enough to finish getting our people into the "promised land". I do appreciate, however, that before I come to join You, Adonai, my last view in this earthly life will be of the panorama of the land You promised long ago to my ancestors, Abraham, Isaac, and Jacob (Israel)--land from.....**Gilead to Dan, and all of Napthtali, the land of** Ephraim **and Manasseh, all of the land of Judah as far as the Western sea,the Negev and the plain of the valley of Jericho the city of palm trees, as far as zoar.** (MJFB (Deut. 34:2,3)

(Music becomes louder and plays during the pause)

God chose Moses to carry out His plan because: *Once God assured him he would provide Aaron and the words he would need to speak to Pharaoh, Moses stepped out in faith and was **obedient**)to God--*

Moses chose obedience and became like our Savior, Yeshua...

(Music)

A NEW IMAGE in Yeshua (Jesus) will be a life of blessing. All the promises of God in the Bible will be ours if we are claiming them in His name.

It isn't easy—He doesn't tell us it will be easy to put Him first; in fact, He warns us:

"If the world hates you, you know that it hated Me before it hated you. If you were of the world, the world would love its own.

"These things I have spoken to you, that in Me you may have peace. In the world you will have tribulation; but be of good cheer, I have overcome the world." (NKJV, John 16:33)

Charles Stanley's comments on verse 33: "How could a man about to be crucified say that He had overcome the world? Jesus overcame the world by obeying His Father despite all challenges and opposition. In a similar way, we too can be overcomers." (NKJV, Rev. 3:21; 12:11)

The good news is that the Son of Man has conquered Satan, sin, and death. He has overcome it all and promises to restore full fellowship and eternal life with God to all who overcome with Him. His victory is ours. We are more than conquerors. We have overcome by the blood of the Lamb and the word of our testimony!" (see Rev.12:11) (Booker, 2011)

Hallelujah!

Jesus will intercede for us today, if we ask, just as Moses did then...

Here's an "Overcomer" who never imagined he could grow to be so much like His Savior, Yeshua:

RANDY

Randy grew up in a small town in Texas, attending church with his family, participating in usual kids' activities throughout elementary school, evincing an interest in science and math in high school, and going on much later to attend college and scattered courses.

While attending church in his teen-age years, some of His teachers' answers to his unwelcome questions during Bible Study didn't seem to match up with what he thought the Bible said. He attended church sporadically after leaving home, then, not at all for many years.

He had a relatively successful business in Lubbock; several people indicated they had a position for him if he ever decided to get out of the headaches of owning a small business. Meanwhile, he "spent 20 years as a heathen"..., in his own words.

Randy eventually did sell his business and inquired around about those openings that had been mentioned before; however, no opportunities seemed to be there at that time.

He met a man who asked him if he would be interested in becoming a Tech.-PR contractor at a place where he knew; which, after much unsuccessful job-shopping and the end of a dis-spiriting and disillusioning short marriage experience, proved to be a satisfactory solution. The move to Carlsbad became God's answer.

Randy feels the Lord closed the doors in Lubbock in order to give him the wonderful opportunity to study and teach Torah, not only in Carlsbad, but also in Hobbs, where an avid group of Torah students are striving to be obedient to God by living the Torah (being in His Image).

"Your belief is entwined with your character," Randy opined, "We are trying to more deeply understand the character of God so we can fulfill God's purpose of being in the "image of Yeshua " (Jesus) every day and every minute of our lives."

(Thanks, Randy, for being a vessel of God, and answering His call for a Torah teacher. The group is very fortunate to have Randy guide the Torah meetings every Friday evening—unabashedly giving the credit to Yeshua for any blessings he brings to the group. He often says he is blessed mightily with the way each one is growing so much closer to our Messhiach, Yeshua, our Savior.)

Upon my visit to another group of "Hebrew Roots" people who have been "called" to study Torah and to become "e-chad" (as "One" in Yeshua), I met a delightful gal whose nickname was Bebe. She has her own story to tell...

Bebe

I used to be Catholic, but sometimes I couldn't understand what was going on; so, oftentimes my mind just wandered. It seemed like something was missing.

One day, my cousin invited me to Bible study at her house. We were talking about this "Missing" feeling, when one of the group said, 'Bebe, come to our congregation—you might find what you are missing in the Torah—the Books of Moses (the first five books of the Bible)—that is what we study, as well as a reading from the Gospel each week.'

My cousin and I went one day. I was so alert and interested—my eyes seemed to be opened to Yeshua, Jesus, our Hebrew Savior. I had never heard of nor seen the Lord in this way! It touched me so; I became very emotional—He talked to me in a different manner—in a personal way.

My other brothers and sisters that go to the congregation helped to satisfy my urge from Him to study the Torah by teaching me also. I remember when stepping into faith in a "personal" Yeshua I cried, my heart was so touched.

He changed my life! I never thought I would get so close to Yeshua, our Savior. It has been about a few years now that I have been going to Congregation, and He has opened my heart and mind in a Way I could never have imagined!

Even though some in my family question why I have left the Catholic way of "worshiping"; it was not for them--I did it for Yeshua; and now I feel whole and peaceful in Him.

(You are so right, Bebe—the Peace that passeth all understanding comes ONLY from Him—Yeshua—Jesus, our Messhiach, our Messiah).

WHY AM I HERE?

If and when we finally get to the point of asking ourselves, "Why am I here?" perhaps we have stopped long enough (or Yeshua has convicted us) to realize that striving to please "self" every day just doesn't "cut it"…There must be more to living a truly fulfilled life than acquiring the "things" of this world…a career, car, house, family…then a better car, a better house, a newer phone, a place in "society" (recognition, either good or bad); or…the "good" causes we join and noisily proclaim our saintly giving of time and money; there MUST BE MORE than this "image" we have developed and portrayed over the years.

Or, perhaps because of our frantic ignorance of what we actually want or need, our agenda becomes that of pleasing the immediate desires of our flesh…looking good to those around us, striving to satisfy a craving for acceptance into some sort of cult or group, or adapting our mores (values) to fit suggested, imagined (movies and TV romanticized versions) physical desires.

The impressions which fill our minds from external sources are what we act on in our lives; so daily prayer, reading scripture, and asking the Holy Spirit to guide us are the only real "armor" we have against those "bad" spirits—walking in the Image of our Lord causes Hasatan (the evil one) to flee from us.

This makes it all the more imperative that we first learn the Word, pray, and exemplify the Truth of His promises to others by our example (in other words, choose Life instead of death.)

Walking like Yeshua becomes our love, joy, and peace all rolled into one!

SOME PERSONAL MIRACLES OF THOSE FINDING A NEW IMAGE IN YESHUA

Two of Harrold's Stories of Triumph in Yeshua Messhiach, Jesus

"It was like landing on a bed of feathers!" Harrold marveled as he told me about God's amazing providence when he was sure he was going to be either killed or at least badly injured.

"My grandmother's farm home was perched on the side of a cliff with a bushy tree and a fence close to the edge of that cliff. My intention was to cut a particularly dense branch from that tree to retrieve the wonderful view of the stream and sky my Grandma previously had before the tree had so lushly leafed out that Spring...an admirable good deed planned; however, the old saying, 'The best-laid plans of mice and men....'

When the ladder was leaned against the tree, my trusty chain saw firmly grasped in my left hand, and a determination not to look over the edge of the not too deep, but quite sheer cliff, I began the ascent. What I thought was going to be easy seemed to become a little more hazardous when my eyes rested on the dried sharp brush under the ladder, left from my brush-clearing of several days before. 'Oh well, I'll just have to be very careful and hang on tight with my free hand,' I thought to myself.

Climbing to the next-to-the-top rung of the ladder (didn't realize the branch was that far up), the chain saw started all right, the limb was almost all the way through, and I was about to give a sigh of relief, when the branch began to fall taking the ladder with it. During that fall, my mind immediately conjured those spikes of dried bush stems piercing my body wherever I hit the ground.

Praise God! There was no way that branch could have gotten underneath my ladder the way it did--except by the Grace of God--and caused my landing to be like landing on a 'bed of feathers.' He was looking after me once again.

Psalm 91:4-6 **He shall cover you with His feathers, and under his wings you shall take refuge; His truth shall be your shield and buckler (seatbelt?), You shall not be afraid of the terror by night, nor of the arrow that flies by day, nor of the pestilence that walks in darkness, nor of the destruction that lays waste at noonday. (my parenthesis)** (NKJV)

Once before, long ago at a young and impetuous age, when squeezed between two vehicles traveling at a fast rate of speed, thinking the crash was inevitable, the Lord guided Harrold's hand on the steering wheel to direct his car into the narrow passage—the only possible space available, which helped Harrold to avoid being in a horrific accident that would have definitely been death for all. He had decided after that he would trust the Lord, Jesus Christ, in any situation. That decision has led Harrold into a personal relationship with Jesus for a Holy-Spirit-inspired life of joy, peace, and righteousness.

JANIE (Sagas of the Lord's protection)

When I first saw Janie, she was on her cell phone talking rather loudly and quite earnestly in a pleading tone of voice, which I couldn't help but overhear, about how to pray and trust in God for the help needed for the couple to save their marriage. She continually repeated how Jesus has promised to answer prayer;   that it was the only thing for them to do, as it was up to the couple to resolve their problems; and that all Janie and her caller could do was to turn the couple over to Jesus and trust in Him for the answer. (I recognized her immediately as a Sister in Christ!)

After Janie hung up, I hugged her and told her that advice was good, and that He would hear their prayers of distress. When she told me that she was talking to her sister, Lisa; and that Lisa had not yet learned to fully trust Jesus, my heart went out to her.

 She began to fill me in about her miraculous conversion and how bad she had been as a teen-ager before that—and how she had married at 14… I knew here was a story for this book—A New Image; because once the Lord got her attention, Janie began to develop that new image—working every day to resume the image we are born into—the image of God, and the need to strive every day to be more like Jesus.

From the time she became aware that her earthly father was beating her Mother, she knew instinctively to stay out of his way. Her mother often put them to bed before he came home. She knew there were bunkbeds in their garage, and that her father brought home "friends" to stay in their garage periodically; that area was off-limits to her and her sisters. One evening, however, John, her father, was searching for money to buy beer. Finding none, his irritation became more and more obvious until he slammed out the back door, relieving all of them for a few precious moments. They didn't even have time to give a sigh of relief, however, when he came back in and ordered her Mom, "Bring all of the girls in here and line them up."

Her Mom called her 16 yr.-old sister, 14 yr.-old sister, Janie, 12, and her younger sister, 8, into the room and put them in stair-step order, wondering what her husband was up to now.

When she heard her husband say to the several men, "Give me $50 and you can take your choice," my mom grabbed a kitchen knife and stepped in front of us girls. She said, "Over my dead body!" and herded us into the house, then into the bedroom and locked the door, checking the window to be sure it was closed and locked. After much pounding on the door, and hearing my Mother shout through the door, "The first one through the door will feel my knife in his throat;" it finally became quiet and my Mother soothed us until we fell asleep despite our terror.

Is it any wonder why Janie embraced the principalities of darkness, began to use foul language, and married at 14? Thankfully, she had been introduced to Yeshua and feels like He came to be with her and in her when, as a child, their whole class had been encouraged to accept Jesus in the Pentacostal church she had been attending, mainly to get out of a house full of immorality.

(Her Mother had succumbed to the wiles of the deceiver, and produced not only one child from the husband of her daughter, who lived in the same house, but a second child—not from her own husband, but again from the husband of her daughter—who chose not to leave her husband and became totally estranged from her Mother even though they lived in the same house).

But, Praise God, Janie found Yeshua (*she feels He has been looking after her all those years ever since her profession of faith when she obeyed her Sunday school teacher and went to the front with her class*) in a more personal way and reads her Bible and communes with Him every day. She is still with her husband of many years, (*who was coaxed away from his budding faith at an early age by Janie, even becoming mixed up in drugs; but, has repented and become the man God had purposed him to be*).

Janie, as a teen-ager, had seduced him from that narrow path to Jesus she had not yet found. She admits she threatened to leave him if he didn't come dancing with her and show her those good times she craved.

When her first baby couldn't breathe, however; and Janie was so devastated by the Doctor's warning, she fell on her knees and promised God she would change…she admitted her sins, asked for forgiveness, and promised God if her baby lived, she would stop smoking, cursing, and being angry, and would learn more about Jesus and strive to be more like Him.

When she saw the Doctor coming toward her with a very serious face, her heart ached; however, before he even reached her, they both heard a baby crying…the doctor turned and literally ran back into the room. Even though she had been forbidden entry, Janie followed him into the room. Her baby was alive! The Doctor was amazed; because he had gone to tell her that her baby had died.

After many tests, the report was that he would be a special needs child because of the 12 minutes of brain-dead time. Today, Janie's son is in the United States Army, played sports all through high school, and found the Lord at a very young age. Janie thanks God for her baby's miracle recovery; and also thanks Him for the guidance of the Holy Spirit for her and her husband every day.

Singing in the choir at Beit Haderick every Shabbat, worshipping our Lord is the inspiration God gives her to praise Him with thanksgiving.

Phyllis's Story...

In answer to my query about any miracles in her life since she had proclaimed Jesus (Yeshua) as her Savior, Phyllis, my cousin by marriage wrote:

"Sept. 25, 2012: **God performs miracles in our lives every day;** but this is one I will always remember:

I had been to the hospital in Des Moines, Iowa, as Robert, my husband, had been taken there because of heart problems he was having. Our daughter, Sheila, met me at the hospital and followed me back to our home in Creston, Iowa.

We were about 10 miles from home, when I realized I was getting very sleepy. I tried concentrating on Bible verses I had committed to memory but drifted off to sleep; when my eyes opened, I was going off the road on the opposite side of the highway.

I immediately said, 'Lord, I can't handle this. You will need to do it!' I remember keeping my hands on the steering wheel and my foot on the accelerator, but I wasn't clearly seeing things around me.

I realized I was riding alongside of the bank, and at one point, when the wheels on the right side of the car left the ground, I remember calmly thinking, 'I could turn over.' The car continued going down the side of the ditch, but I wasn't really seeing clearly what was going on. Everything was kind of a blur. I remember the car coming back up on the highway and the wheels doing a lot of screeching; and then realized I was back on the highway on my side of the road and seeing clearly. I very calmly drove the rest of the way home and parked the car in the garage.

I don't think I really comprehended what had happened until Sheila parked behind me and ran up to me and said, 'Mom, you will never know how helpless I felt!' She was honking at me to try and get me to stop the car, but not once did I hear her doing that. It was then I began to think back to what really happened. I was not driving that car, the minute I said to the Lord, 'I can't handle this,' He took over and that is why everything around me was kind of a blur to me. This is why I didn't turn over when the wheels left the ground on one side of the car. The screeching noise I heard as I came back up on the pavement had to be the car straightening out as I came out of the ditch. I am a person who gets very excited when my husband will maybe let the wheels of the car leave the highway for a second. With God being at my side and taking over—that accounts for my calmness through all of this including my driving home as though nothing had ever happened.

This was nothing but a miracle. Some people have a hard time believing this really happened; but my daughter witnessed the entire scene from behind me. I have praised my Lord many times as I think back to that day and all He protected me from. Also, this was a road that had a lot of traffic on it and that day, not one car was on the road until I got closer to my home.

This miracle is something that is hard for me to describe to people as I was aware of what was going on but I wasn't clearly seeing what was happening.

OUT OF THE MOUTHS OF BABES...

Several weeks later, I was teaching my Joy class of 4-6 yr.-olds on God hearing and answering our prayer. I mentioned to them that I had gone into the ditch not too long ago and how God had heard and answered my prayer and protected me and brought me back up to the highway. The next week one of the little girl's father came to me and told me that he and his daughter were on a slick road that week and he said to his daughter, 'I hope we don't go in the ditch.' His daughter said to him, 'Dad, if we do, it's o.k. because Mrs. Gideon went into the ditch and God just drove her right out of it.' Yes, I did relate the miracle that had happened to me to him and his wife!"

CARMI's Story

When she was six, the miracle she saw was nothing unusual. She thought everyone had these kind of supernatural happenings. Her "Momma" (actually her Grandma), who raised her along with Grandpa, was a woman of strong faith in Jesus (Yeshua), always prayed about everything, and believed her Father in heaven would answer her prayers.

That day, however, in hindsight, was a really big miracle...at least for her Uncle, who was about 16 years old and had been out in his workshop sawing something. Carmi and Grandma were on the sun porch—Carmi, playing with her dolls; Grandma, sewing something, when they heard a frantic yelling coming toward the back door.

Grandma was on her feet and about to the middle of the sunroom when Uncle burst through the door to meet Grandma, hollering and holding up his hand with one finger dangling by one thin piece of skin.

Grandma immediately grasped the hand tightly, squeezing the finger into proper position and held onto the hand while both of them were talking to the Lord asking Him for healing of that finger. Their prayers became louder and more earnest than ever while Grandma hung on for "dear life."

Carmi wasn't old enough to realize just how much time went by (seemed like a long time) or to recollect most of the details...all she remembers is that when Grandma finally let loose of his hand, there was no blood on the attached finger he held up, and he was no longer moaning and groaning in pain. When Grandma looked at her own hand, it was filled with Uncle's blood, as was the floor beneath their feet.

"My 'Momma's' faith was a true picture of God's love, mercy, and compassion; and I praise God for her Godly example during my growing-up years. The only time I remember going to the Doctor all those years was the time my leg was broken, and it was my grandpa who insisted he take me there. Any sniffles or sore throats, or colds were taken care of with home remedies like: for stomach ache—ate a slice of raw potato; a cold—suck on a burned-out match, rubbed mentholatum on chest and bottom of feet; then put socks on and went to bed. There were many more old-time "cures," but I've forgotten most.

Momma would say, "It's a poor mechanic who could build a car and couldn't fix it; and God is not a poor mechanic...He built you and He can sure fix you!'"

Carmi constantly praises God for giving her that Godly Grandmother to be her Mother and Mentor; and gives her the credit for leading her into the Family of God. "Even my 97 year-old Aunt, who just recently was saved, will be quick to admit our family is still benefitting from Momma's prayers!"

Carol's Latest Miracle:
Proof that your daily prayers are important:

Praise God for the latest miracle in my life and in the life of my youngest granddaughter! Being new in town and finally going to school in person, as the school systems in Colorado are, she had met only one girl and was leaving at lunchtime with her to get a quick lunch at a local fast food hangout for high school kids. The car that offered them a lift was driven by a "friend" of Grace's friend, who indicated she knew him and that they might as well ride with him instead of taking her car. The situation was such that Grace felt no trepidation—middle of the day—only two blocks to the restaurant—what could go wrong??--not! Her friend took the front passenger seat—Grace in the backseat behind her.

A speeding "clunker" whizzed by evidently sparking an ember of a previous contest—the race was on! The two-car, one pickup crash was bad enough to have killed everyone involved; the worst injury was of the woman driving the pickup, who was an innocent driver simply running an errand downtown.

Every teen involved was injured, some badly, except my grand-daughter, who was in the backseat behind her "friend." My granddaughter had passed out; and when the others saw the car was catching fire, they pulled her out. Her Mother was devastated when she saw Grace in the neckbrace at the hospital, thinking, praying, "Please, Lord, not a spinal injury!"

However, after all tests, Praise God, nothing was broken, no concussion, and a valuable lesson learned (we pray so) by my teen granddaughter. The whole family gave thanks to God for His hedge of protection that we all try to remember to pray for our family in our daily prayers—especially for our teen-age high schooler! (Psalm 91) The EMT said Grace's seatbelt was what saved her...our family knew it was our Lord Who watches over her Who saved our Grace!

Heather's Miracle

And then there is Heather, who had that same sweet, tender, loving look in her eyes that I have noticed in all the people who have told me a story of God's special love and providence revealed to them....

Heather is from Moore, Oklahoma, a town hit by a second record-setting tornado in just a few years—a town so blessed otherwise that most would not even think of relocating—a town, in the most instances filled with a loving, caring inspired-by-God population.

This last tornado—a 5-point storm—included an elementary school in its path, and was devastating in its entirety; however, Heather was able to say, "In this one area—a "U" shaped inclusion of a section of three streets was missed completely by the wrath of the funnel-shaped whirlwind that was said to have cut a swathe a mile wide and, in most cases, straight through the town, seemingly intent on flattening everything in its path.

Trying not to panic, Heather, in her schoolroom, saw to it that her students (and some parents who were able to get there within the short warning time they had—about 15 minutes) were against the most central wall, on their hands and knees, arms covering head, leaning head down as close to the floor as possible—just as they had practiced many times in their routinely daily end-of-the-day activities.

When the all-clear finally sounded, everyone dazedly went back to their desks and sat quietly waiting for further instructions....

Several days later, feeling guilty for being so happy her school and her house had been on the short part of the street that met the cross street that formed that "U" of the only surviving area of the storm, Heather's question was finally answered.

I'll call him John--a tall, imposing man of God from the country of Trinidad, who lived across the street from Heather had stepped out into the middle of their street with the "twister" coming straight for where he was standing, with fist in the air, said loudly and firmly, "I tell you TURN AWAY, tornado, in the name of Jesus!"

Surprisingly, not to John, but to others who were watching, the storm turned and left that area without a scratch. Faith in God is a powerful weapon even against the elements: (since God controls them, your prayers "availeth much," especially if you are in His will).

John 14:13-14 **"And I will do whatever you ask in my name, so that the Son may bring glory to the Father. You may ask me for anything in my name, and I will do it."** (NIV)

THERE IS NOTHING IN THIS WORLD LIKE IT! Praying for His DNA to replace mine in every cell of my body has been an explosive experience—a literal taking on of the IMAGE OF GOD and the knowledge that, Spiritually, He has been there always, since being born in His Image;

however, it took me many years to acknowledge Him as my heart, mind, soul, and being—extensions of His power and glory—answerable only to Him and responsible for glorifying His Holy name by trying to be holy as He is holy.

*Dr. Mike Evans defines DNA not only with the scientific definition... "deoxyribonucleic acid, the molecule that contains your genetic code," but in his book LIVING IN THE F.O.G., he uses the definition, "**Divine Nature Acquired**." (Evans, 2012)*

"Not only are we created by God, it is through Him that we live, and move, and have our being. It is because of His DNA that you can have a significant life. Because He loves you, God's Spirit directs you as you walk in His favor." (Evans, 2012)

(louder music building up, but when reader comes in, be sure music does not drown out the reader!)

(Read this last paragraph slowly, emphasize each word amd pause with much expression and feeling)

A New Image—a living, breathing, Yeshua, reflected in us and through us for those around us to see, bask in, and soak up-- a "pure" Oxygen type of love that is our purpose in Adonai… to do His will and to live a daily life reflecting His love, goodness, and mercy. Wow! Worth striving toward? AB-SO-LUTE-LY!

(Not necessary to read outloud, but have same Bibliography as physical book)

Bibliography

Booker, D. R. (2011). *The Overcomers.* Destiny Image Publishers.

CLBriggs--168

Christopher D. Hudson, D. B. (n.d.). *365 Daily Readings from Biblical History.* Barbour Publishing Inc.

Enarson, L. (2009). *The Feasts of the Lord.* Ariel Media.

Evans, M. (2012). *Living in the F.O.G.* **Timeworthy Books.**

Fischer, J. (2009). *Kid's Bible Dictionary.* Barbour Publishing Inc.

Howard, M. (2004). *Love Constrained.* Out of Africa Publishers.

Life Application Study Bible, NIV. (2005). Zondervan Publishing Inc.

MacArthur, J. (2006). *MacArthur Study Bible, NASB.* Thomas Nelson Inc

Messianic Jewish Family Bible, Tree of Life Version, (c) 2014, by the Messianic Jewish Family Bible Society.

Michael, B. (2013). *God-Fearers.* FFOZ Publishing.

Precept Ministries. (1992,1993). *The International Inductive Study Bible, NASB.* Harvest House Publishers.

Scott, S. K. (2010).*The Greatest Words Ever Spoken.* Waterbrook Press.

Sproul, R. C. (n.d.). The Holiness of God. *Tabletalk Magazine.*

Stamps, D. C., & Adams, J. W. (1992). *Full Life Study Bible, NIV.* Zondervan Publishing House.

Stanley, C. (2012, March). *In Touch Magazine*, p. P. 4.

Stanley, C. (2012, July). *In Touch Magazine*, p. 5 and 40.

Stanley, C. F. (2005). *Life Principles Bible, NKJV.* **Thomas Nelson Pub**.

Stern, D. H. (1998). *Complete Jewish Bible.* Messianic Jewish Publishing.

Welker, C. (2007,2008). *Should Christians be Torah Observant.* Netzari Press.

Young, S. (2004,2011).JESUS CALLING, Enjoying Peace in His Presence. Thomas Nelson Inc.

CLBriggs

CPSIA information can be obtained
at www.ICGtesting.com
Printed in the USA
BVHW082215280321
603591BV00006B/1017